Summary

Of

Happy Gut

The Cleansing Program to Help You Lose Weight, Gain Energy, and Eliminate Pain

By Vincent Pedre

Summarized by Scorpio Digital Press

The information in the following pages is broadly considered a truthful and accurate account of facts and as such, any inattention, use, or misuse of the information in question by the reader will render any resulting actions solely under their purview. There are no scenarios in which the publisher or the original author of this work can be in any fashion deemed liable for any hardship or damages that may befall them after undertaking information described herein.

Additionally, the information in the following pages is intended only for informational purposes and should thus be thought of as universal. As befitting its nature, it is presented without assurance regarding its prolonged validity or interim quality. Trademarks that are mentioned are done without written consent and can in no way be considered an endorsement from the trademark holder.

Table of Contents

Book Summary of Happy Gut

The Cleansing Program to assist You change state, Gain Energy, and Eliminate Pain

Happy Gut delves into the way to cleanse your gut of poisons from displcasing and unhealthy foods that area unit leading to a leaky gut and inflammation in your region. Dr. Pedre discusses however feeding lean, organic meats, and lots of fresh vegetables helped improve how he felt overall and lays out how it can work for you. Getting obviate processed foods and cookery meals reception will improve your energy levels and general well-being. First and foremost, conquering your unhappy gut involves understanding why your gut is performing below its optimal level.

Part I covers however you bought to wherever you're and the way your gut was thrown out of balance. It talks about what foods are troublesome and why. Through the Gut C.A.R.E. Program's 28-day program, you can lose weight and eliminate food allergies and sensitivities from your diet without bothering to count calories. You'll have to be compelled to avoid bound foods for an extended amount of your time however you may successively feel awake and energized whereas losing weight.

Part II is on the gut bring up system of the program that teaches you ways to mend your unruly gut. Dr. Pedre provides you tips for achievement whereas on the program and answers several usually asked queries.

Part III explores the way to re-introduce foods into your diet that you simply removed throughout those twenty eight days. Through an individualized plan combining the best of both Eastern and Western medicine, you will get back to your fully functioning self by discovering the underlying symptoms of your gut ailments. This arrange can facilitate guide you thru life once you're through with the Gut C.A.R.E. Program. Part IV looks at the emotional and physical connections to overall gut health. An unhealthy gut will adversely have an effect on your mood and cause depression, attention deficit disorder, and even autism. To achieve overall well-being, one must align the body, mind, and spirit. The gut acts as a second brain that talks to your brain and it's imperative that you simply hear your gut as a result of it's instinctual. Alternative modalities like treatment and massage will facilitate maintain a healthy gut. Yoga can also promote a happy gut. Dr. Pedre finishes with recipes to take care of a healthy gut and concludes with useful tools and resources to assist you get through the program.

PART I: IT'S ALL ABOUT THE GUT

Chapter 1: It's All in Your Gut

Part I covers how the gut was thrown out of balance, what these imbalances do to you, and which foods are the worst for your gut and why. Chapter 1 digs into the imbalance of the gut and lays out the Gut C.A.R.E. Program that can be implemented during a 28 day time period. A healthy gut, according to Dr. Pedre: has all food digested into its component parts, a vibrant digestive surface that adequately absorbs micronutrients form health foods while blocking larger, partially digested food particles, bacteria, and yeast, and the immune system of the gut activates only when necessary, remaining not overworked. The gut has five main roles: digestion of food, absorption of nutrients, maintenance of an immune barrier, a symbiotic relationship with favorable bacteria, and detoxification that readily removes waste and toxins from the body.

Western medicine regularly treats the symptoms of a malady rather than their causes. Western doctors regularly call gut problems IBS (irritable bowl syndrome), while failing to get to the root causes of the problem. We are what we eat. "The foods we eat control our state of health, and the gut is the gateway to the rest of the body," Dr. Pedre writes. But here's the good news: YOU are in control of what you put in your body.

Eating the wrong foods puts toxins into your system resulting in dysbiosis, which, if left untreated, will develop into a leaky gut. This leaky gut exposes the body to partially digested protein from food that the immune system does not recognize, so it attacks them, leading to food sensitivities, manifesting themselves as hives, allergies, inflammation, and migraines. Leaky gut is a process that has numerous factors that has no known cure other than a strict and healthy diet. It is essentially a condition that loosens the connections of cells that line the intestines, allowing larger molecules to pass through the gut wall. Two of the top five most deadly cancers in the world are gastrointestinal (stomach cancer is 3rd and colon cancer is 4th).

Dr. Pedre's Gut C.A.R.E Program stands for: Cleanse, Activate, Restore, and Enhance. C.A.R.E also means caring for your gut through a three-pronged mind, body, spirit approach. It aims to reboot your system through a restoration of balance to your digestive tract that brings about total body wellness. If you follow the C.A.R.E.

template, you will "reestablish gut happiness." Furthermore, "By following the Happy Gut Diet, balance is restored to the gut and inflammation is reversed. And, by fixing the gut, we accomplish much more than just a reduction in gut-associated inflammation; we fix inflammation everywhere in the body."

Cleansing removes gut irritants, infections, and toxins from your food.

Activating sparks a healthy digestion by replacing essential nutrients and enzymes.

Restoration involves reintroducing beneficial bacteria for your healthy gut.

Enhancing repairs, regenerates, and heals the intestinal lining.

Record your key health events and symptoms. Then fill out the Happy Gut Pre-Program Symptoms Questionnaire to help track how you feel different over this 28 day process.

Chapter 2: The Happy Gut Diet: Phase I Explained

This chapter details what foods you can eat and which foods you cannot eat on the Happy Gut Diet. First and foremost, do NOT eat sugar. This includes anything with high-fructose corn syrup or any other sweeteners. Sugar is craved and it does initially satisfy this craving, spiking your blood pressure and heart rate, making you feel energized. Soon thereafter though, your insulin levels start to rise and control the blood sugar level, resulting in a drop in blood sugar. This makes you feel irritable, angry, inpatient, and easily annoyed. Then you feel tired or achy. Cortisol is secreted to stabilize your blood sugar and high cortisol stresses your adrenals and winds you up. This makes you feel panicked, anxious, and unsettled. So, your brain tells you that you need another hit of sugar. And on the roller coaster ride goes.

Sugar is bad for you because: it is unsustainable energy and absent of any essential nutrients, vitamins or proteins. Sugar is high in fructose which can overload the liver and lead you to want to eat more, too much sugar can lead to a fatty liver or metabolic disease and fibrosis of the liver. Sugar can cause insulin resistance, leading to metabolic syndrome and eventually heart disease or diabetes. It also causes inflammation and pain, increases one's body weight no matter how old you are, is highly addictive (like a drug), feeds cancer, and raises one's cholesterol.

Don't drink diet sodas on the Happy Gut Diet. Research revealed that drinkers of diet sodas experience a 70 percent greater increase in waist circumference than non-diet soda drinkers. Why avoid diet soda? They make you gain weight. They increase your risk of stroke or heart attack or cardiovascular disease. They overstimulate your sweet receptors so you can't appreciate natural sweeteners in foods like fruit. Phosphoric acid in diet sodas leaches calcium from your bones, which can lead to weak bones and fractures.

You must also cut out gluten from your diet because it is just as addicting as sugar. Gliadorphin, a protein from gluten, mimics the effects of opiates. The food industry has hijacked your brain to want more gluten by creating a wheat plant with up to 50 percent more gluten in it than it did a half century ago. Up to 30 percent of the

U.S. population has a sensitivity to gluten and 2 percent have developed celiac disease. Research has also shown that people can become sensitive to gluten without developing autoimmune celiac disease. If you remove gluten from your diet, monitor what changes occur. It will take up to two weeks to notice the changes but after four weeks your improvement in overall health will be apparent. Gluten-free foods include amaranth, arrowroot, and garbanzo beans. Gluten products are barley, bulgur, cakes, and cereals. It is very likely that gluten may be slowing down your metabolism, interfering with your thyroid function which can lead to thyroid disease, weight gain, and difficulty losing weight. Gluten-free foods are not necessarily healthier for you however.

Instead, Dr. Pedre advises to eat whole foods with lean or healthy fat proteins, slow carbs, non-starchy vegetables, nuts, and seeds. Eating gluten-free foods filled with “sugar equivalents” (SE) will only feed your sugar addiction. The best gluten-free alternatives are: avocados, arugula, artichokes, all varieties of berries, baby romaine, and sweet potatoes.

Milk and dairy should be avoided. Soy milk is not a valid substitute. Some rice milk has gluten. Homemade almond or cashew milk is best. Coconut milk from the store can contain the corrosive carrageenan. Sugar-free hemp milk works as it is a solid source of omega-3 fats. A dairy-free diet not only helps your digestive system, it can also give you healthy, vibrant, glowing skin. Milk does not in and of itself keep your bones strong. This is evidenced by a Western world that drinks milk while recording the highest rates of osteoporosis (brittle and fragile bones). In addition, "The same way that gluten metabolizes into an opiate-like substance, so does the protein casein found in milk and other dairy products."

Eggs can be dangerous because the food hens are fed can be a diet of soy and corn. It's not good for the hens and it is not good for us. Organic eggs from cage-free hens fed a natural diet of omega-3 fats are much better. The best eggs can be found at your local farmers market. Soy is also everywhere and it interferes with the absorption of essential minerals. It can also trigger issues with your thyroid. Corn is a high-glycemic food that will spike one's blood sugar similar to the way cane sugar does. It is a SE food that is just as harmful to us as sugar. Legumes such as alfalfa, beans, carob, lentils, peas, soybeans, and peanuts are high in lectins so they also pose similar problems as the foods previously mentioned: causing inflammation and weight gain. Legumes are also known for causing gas, leading to bloating, causing abdominal pain, and creating discomfort.

"Nightshade" includes a group of vines, herbs, shrubs, and trees such as mandrake, belladonna, and tobacco. Examples are tomatoes, eggplant, potatoes, and bell peppers. Nightshades are a "particular source of agony for many people who suffer from arthritic conditions or autoimmune disorders." These plants produce alkaloids, which can be toxic to humans if ingested in large amounts or taken by those who are particularly sensitive to tiny amounts. Like gluten, they contain sugar-binding proteins that activate the immune system and result in inflammation and pain. Dr. Pedre strongly recommends removing the above-mentioned foods from your diet during the 28 day "Elimination Phase."

He ends with a Happy Gut Shopping List including what is in and what is out for: vegetables, fruit, dairy, grains, meat/fish, nuts/seeds, vegetable proteins, fats/oils, drinks, sweeteners, and condiments.

PART II: THE GUT C.A.R.E. PROGRAM:

TWENTY-EIGHT DAYS TO A NEW YOU

Chapter 3: Eliminate Symptoms and Maintain Your Gut With the Gut C.A.R.E Program

The second part of Happy Gut begins to speak to how you heal your gut with Dr. Pedre's gut "reboot" system called the Gut C.A.R.E. Program. Chapter three details the overview of this diet and includes a step-by-step plan for how to fix your diet and calm any discomfort you feel by changing what you eat.

C.A.R.E. is a gut reboot system that is a way to restore and repair your gut to its normal and natural functioning. It will help reestablish balance in your system, benefitting your entire body. It will take at least two weeks for the body to heal from your previous diet and will take another two weeks to start to feel the effects of the Gut C.A.R.E. Program. C.A.R.E. is also about self-care, being kind to yourself by focusing on what you are actually putting into your body. Eating is a ritual and should not be something you scarf down in between your endless stream of tasks to complete during the day.

The CLEANSE process removes the harmful substances from your body by eating the right foods and removing the ones that contribute to poor gut health. In addition, replace harmful thoughts with gratitude, cleansing clears out all that is detrimental to your body. To truly cleanse means to totally avoid both coffee and alcohol. You can eat organic/non-GMO food, nuts, seeds, healthy fats, high-fiber/low-glycemic carbs, non-starchy vegetables, hypoallergenic proteins (peas, rice, chia, hemp), clean/lean proteins (free-range chicken/turkey, hormone-free beef/lamb, wild-caught cold-water fish). Implement your CLEANSE routine daily by: eliminating all high-sensitivity foods mentioned in Chapter 2, take the Gut C.A.R.E. supplement three times a day before meals, prepare the Gut C.A.R.E. CLEANSE SHAKE (see smoothie recipes in Chapter 9) three times a day before meals, drink clean water, create a greener kitchen, cleanse your mind, and express daily gratitude.

ACTIVATE aims to reactivate the healthy function of the gut by remedying deficiencies in the digestive process by using supplements that replenish what it is lacking. This activation of your digestive system will improve the breakdown of proteins, fats, and carbs. You can implement ACTIVATE daily by starting with a Gut C.A.R.E. Program ACTIVATE digestive enzyme three times a day before meals, add a betaine HCI (acid supplement), start everyday with a Happy Gut breakfast smoothie with raw/enzyme rich foods, work with a medical practitioner to figure out any specific areas that need addressing in your body, and take the Gut C.A.R.E. Relax supplement before bed each night.

RESTORE's purpose is to use probiotics and prebiotics to reinoculate the intestines with friendly flora. This process is designed to "reestablish microbial balance in your gut ecosystem," thereby reintroducing "the favorable bacteria, or probiotics, that were decimated by all types of gut insults, most notably antibiotics, unfavorable bacterial infections, parasites, and yeast." Probiotics help improve gut immunity. They not only protect against pathogens, they also help reduce the leakiness of the gut and bolster the immune system. Foods to incorporate to help protect you and get your probiotics are: cultured foods (yogurts or kefir 13), fermented foods (vegetables, sauerkraut, kimchi), and cultured beverages containing live bacteria (kombucha, coconut water kefir). However, it is still best to avoid dairy entirely for the first 28 days.

Top foods with prebiotics are raw chicory root, raw Jerusalem artichoke, raw dandelion greens, raw garlic, raw leeks, and raw onions. Many of these contain soluble fibers that are important because they attract water and delay the emptying of the stomach. Apples, beans, blueberries, carrots, celery, cucumbers, nuts, oranges, and strawberries are all great sources for soluble fiber. Insoluble fibers are also needed to provide bulk to the stool and prevent constipation. Insoluble fibers are found in broccoli, brown rice, carrots, celery, dark/leafy greens, green beans, whole grains, and zucchini.

To implement RESTORE into your daily life: start with a high-potency probiotic everyday, look for dairy-free probiotics and take on an empty stomach twice a day for at least three months, incorporate prebiotic foods into your diet, add cultured foods, incorporate nine servings of fruits and vegetables daily, and eat from the phytonutrient spectrum.

ENHANCE repairs, regenerates, and heals your intestinal lining. This final step of the C.A.R.E. Program's purpose is to repair any damage done to one's gut lining. Enhancement will complete this process by "restoring the integrity of the tight junctions between the cells of the intestinal lining to keep partially digested food particles, toxins, and microbes from 'leaking' into the bloodstream." Implementing ENHANCE daily includes: starting with an L-glutamine supplement powder mixed with water once daily, drink a shot of aloe vera juice every morning, take an omega-3 supplement once a day, and if you have any other discomfort in your body make sure to remedy it with the proper supplements.

A daily life in the Gut C.A.R.E. Program incorporating all four steps will help one live a happy and healthy life. First thing in the morning, wake up and set your intention and emphasize gratitude from the moment you open your eyes. Spend up to ten minutes on yoga and breathing exercises. Meditate for five minutes or so. Drink lemon water. For breakfast, have a morning shake with protein powder and supplements. Lunch should be a meal with Happy Gut-approved foods with a healthy balance of protein, vegetables, and fats. For snacks: raw/steamed vegetables, nuts and seeds, green apple wedges, and hummus with raw carrots.

Dinner is a meal with the proper foods mentioned on the Happy Gut list, recipes can be found in Chapter 9 and should include a protein with a sizable salad or a side of vegetables. If you need a late night snack, go for a bowl of berries, celery sticks with nut butter or apple wedges with nut butter. After each meal, try to take a five to ten minute walk. And try to end each day with a ten or fifteen minute meditation before going to bed.

Chapter 4: Tips for Success: Creating a Happy Gut

This chapter gives you Dr. Pedre's tips for success while on the program with a list of common questions and answers. The first three to seven days will bc the hardest as you cut out the highly sensitive foods from your diet and adjust to the Happy Gut Diet. Dr. Pedre lays out the first two weeks of meal planning with three meals a day and optional snacks. During the first week of the program, you will possibly experience detox symptoms from not eating the foods that you were previously digesting. Start off your mornings with a Gut C.A.R.E. morning breakfast smoothie, helping restore the function of your liver, kidneys, and intestines. During this time, you will be removing toxins from your body while also getting rid of excess water retained from inflammation. This will all allow you to naturally lose weight without counting calories.

Slow down when you eat. Take in the conversation with who you are eating with and be in a mindful state when you sit down at the dinner table. "Eating in conscious, positive engagement with others permits you to savor the flavors, and it promotes the internal relaxation that stimulates the digestive process so it can run smoothly." Also, divide your plate into four quarters, filling one with protein and healthy omega-3 fats or meats, then fill the other three-quarters with greens and vegetables. In addition, do not let your food touch the edge of your plate, focusing on eating smaller portions. Stick to the 1:3 ratio of protein to vegetables and you will be on your way. Avoid drinking too much when you eat. Try to drink water between meals because drinking while eating can dilute your stomach acid. This will all make digesting food easier on your body. Still drink at least 64 ounces or eight glasses of water per day but try to drink them before or between meals.

When eating, learn how to recognize when you are 75 percent full and stop eating a few bites after that. Then, wait a minute or two to see if you are actually still hungry. Most times, you will realize that you are actually full. When enmeshed in the Gut C.A.R.E. Program, also ensure to reduce stress. Stress adds inflammation to your body regardless of how healthy you're eating. It activates the fight-or-flight instinctual response that makes you feel like you are under attack when in reality you are not. Stress can also spike your blood pressure, result in palpitations, and reduce blood flow to the intestines, impacting digestion and proper assimilation of nutrients.

After completion of the 28-day Happy Gut Diet, you can begin the Reintroduction Phase where you challenge yourself with foods not included in the diet. If the foods reintroduced cause you problems, Dr. Pedre advises, then go back on the Happy Gut Diet for three to six months.

PART III: REINTRODUCTION PHASE AND FURTHER TESTING

Chapter 5: Reintroduction and Your Gut C.A.R.E. Plan for Life

In this chapter, Dr. Pedre explores the post–Happy Gut Diet phase transitioning into the food Reintroduction Phase. He looks at how to get back to a normal diet after the initial 28 days while also giving you tools to manage your gut with a sustainable and achievable lifelong plan. In this Reintroduction Phase, you will start adding back the foods you were not eating in Phase I.

Reintroduce the foods in the following order:

1. organic, free range eggs (start with boiled, poached or steamed sunny-side up eggs or egg white omelets);
2. organic, rBGH-free dairy (plain yogurt and kefirs);
3. non-GMO corn;
4. non-GMO fermented soy;
5. legumes;
6. wheat/gluten.

Start eating one of these foods every four days. If adverse symptoms (tired, achy, stiff) begin to occur within the first 36 hours, then put that food back into the "avoid" list. If you do not experience any symptoms after reintroducing one of these six types of foods, then introduce another item and give yourself two days to wait for any reactions to come. Repeat this process but don't add more than two items per week.

It is important to keep your regular doctor or a nutritionist in the loop when embarking on this new diet. It is also necessary to remember that the gut changes over time depending on what you eat. Dr. Pedre's cleansing program is meant to empower you to change your diet and change how you feel. However, there will be times when you feel better after taking out some of these sensitive foods from your diet. Staying on the Happy Gut Diet cleansing program twice a hear should help you reboot your system and keep it running on tip-top shape.

Chapter 6: Further Testing for Gut-Related Ailments

This chapter takes a look at the causes and symptoms for common and uncommon gut ailments. It guides your future program beyond the Gut C.A.R.E Program. The tests detailed in this chapter are to help you further refine and guide you toward gut and total body wellness. This is meant to be a reference to use as you work with your health practitioner when you have troubling symptoms.

Here are ten common and not-so-common tests everyone should have, according to Dr. Pedre.

Complete Blood Count: tests for white and red blood cell characteristics and platelet count. Another is Iron Profile with Ferritin: this is a test to measure iron deficiency. Low ferritin reveals that your iron count is low in your body. High ferritin means you likely have inflammation.

Fasting Glucose: this measures how much sugar is present in your body. If your level is more than 216 mg/dl then you are diabetic.

Complete Metabolic Profile: this measure electrolytes, liver, and kidney function. Amylase/Lipase: a tool to find inflammation of the pancreas. An elevated amount of amylase or lipase can mean that something is injuring your pancreas. Insulin Level: when you eat too much sugar or starches, insulin is secreted, leading to insulin resistance and storage of fat around your belly.

Thyroid Function Tests: a sluggish thyroid can lead to hair loss, brittle nails, constipation, and dry skin.

Thyroid Antibodies: these tests are valuable to do when changing your diet.

Vitamin D: a very important hormone to regulate the immune response and increasing calcium absorption in the gut.

Trace Minerals: zinc, selenium, and magnesium. If you have low blood cell levels, increase your dietary sources.

The remainder of this chapter is a guide to testing based on the symptoms you have and ways your gut may have become dysfunctional. With each symptom or condition, tests to consider are offered. The symptoms and conditions include: asthma, allergies, eczema, hives, autoimmune disease, bloating/excessive gas, chronic diarrhea, loose stools, constipation, fatigue, fibromyalgia, muscle pain, fullness immediately after eating, inflammatory bowel disease, IBS, leaky gut syndrome, migraines, nutrient/vitamin deficiencies, sour stomach/acid reflux, yeast overgrowth, and therapeutic interventions.

Dr. Pedre then discusses in detail:

Food intolerances (a result of digestive enzyme deficiency), food allergies (causes an immediate response within seconds or minutes such as skin rash, hives, itching, or an asthma attack), food sensitivities (a prolonged or delayed reaction to food making the problem-causing foods hard to identify), leaky gut syndrome (symptoms overlap with food sensitivity's and there is no perfect test for the syndrome instead relying solely on a doctor's diagnosis, the most objective measure is a positive intestinal permeability test). Gluten intolerance vs. celiac disease and lactose intolerance vs. dairy sensitivity is then discussed.

Other topics finishing out the chapter are: FODMAPs (fermentable, oligo, di, monosaccharides, and polyols), dysbiosis (a common disorder of the gastrointestinal tract), SIBO (small intestine bacterial overgrowth, a type of dysbiosis), candidiasis/yeast overgrowth (forms of a yeast-predominant dysbiosis), functional gut imbalances (disruptions in how the gut performs its daily functions), acid reflux/indigestion (acid indigestion, heartburn, excessive burping, gas, and bloating), Helicobater pylori infection (if you have symptoms of a stomach ulcer including nausea, vomiting, belching, indigestion, and abdominal pain), low stomach acid (food sits undigested in your stomach longer, increasing the likelihood that pressure in your abdomen will push the food upward), digestive enzyme deficiencies (enzymes are needed to break down the food we eat), pancreatic enzyme insufficiency (the pancreas performs important digestive enzymes to break down proteins and fat), medication-induced GI distress (medications can have adverse effects and problematic side effects).

PART IV: A HAPPY GUT, HAPPY LIFE

Chapter 7: The Emotional Gut: The Mind-Gut Connection

The fourth and final part of Happy Gut takes a look at the emotional and physical connections to gut health, discussing how an unhealthy gut can lead to many psychological disorders like depression, attention deficit disorder, and autism. Dr. Pedre outlines how an alignment of the mind, body, and spirit is necessary for lasting health and longevity, sharing simple and effective strategies that have worked for his patients.

Chapter 7 details how the mind-gut connection acts as our second brain. It can be useful in combatting depression and other detrimental conditions. Alternative methods outside of diet are also discussed. "Nothing could be more critical than getting the word out about the connection between seemingly invisible gluten sensitivity and brain dysfunction," Dr. David Perlmutter wrote in the Grain Brain and is the quote Dr. Pedre starts this chapter off with.

Your gut can also affect your mind-state. Treating gut imbalances can not only help your pain and allergies and weight gain from an unhealthy diet, it can also battle brain-related disorders and depression. The gut is the second brain because it also affects your mood and the way your brain functions. The gut, like the brain, has its own nervous system, called the enteric nervous system (ENS). The ENS has a handful of important functions: it coordinates the contraction of muscle cells lining the intestines to keep everything moving in the right direction, it triggers the release of gut hormones and enzymes to promote proper digestion, it helps open up circulation to the gut after eating, and it controls the gut-associated lymphatic immune system. All these functions are communicated to the brain through the autonomic nervous system. This two-way communication can make you have a "nervous" stomach due to the feelings emanating from your mind. Therefore, gut imbalances can trigger behavioral, emotional, and psychiatric symptoms.

A patient-centered approach of Functional Medicine helps treat the root causes of the problem that are regularly missed by Western medical strategies. Improving your gut will in turn affect your brain health. The following factors affect brain health through the gut: bacteria or yeast that produces neurotoxins slowing your ability to think and remember (dysbiosis), all conditions that lead to a leaky gut, the gut immune response to partially digested food proteins that get through the gut lining like gluten, chronic gut inflammation that can lead to the release of signals from the gut's immune system to affect the function of the brain contributing to depression, and a diet rich in starches resulting in the growth of gut bacterial that can damage brain cells. When your gut is out of balance a chain reaction of events can interfere with your brain's proper functioning. That gut feeling you have is real. It is that intuitive sense that you should do something or avoid doing something. Your gut is connected to your anxiety or excitement concerning an upcoming event. "Our gut feelings are the most powerful ally we have to guide us, protect us, and help us navigate through the complexities of life." So you have to learn to "listen to your gut," so you can be steered in the right direction and do what is best for you, Dr. Pedre concludes.

Here is how you can listen to your gut: practice deep listening and pay attention to what is being said by others, meditate and bring mindfulness into every aspect of your life, learn to trust your inner voice, breathe to create inner peace, find your center in stressful situations through yoga and meditation, and practice acceptance.

Stress can be alleviated through a regular meditation practice. It is a powerful tool to promote peace in both your mind and your body. You cannot control external factors but you can control what state of mind you are in. Worrying and getting angry get you nowhere. Meditation relaxes you and your gut while promoting digestion. It puts your ego aside and brings a compassionate detachment into your life. By focusing on your breathing and being alive, you center your mind and calm yourself, focusing not on the suffering present in your life, but on what you have through peace, acceptance, and gratitude. A five to ten minute meditation to get your day started is a critical part of the Gut C.A.R.E. Program.

Other remedies include massage therapy, neuromuscular release (a gentle, targeted massage releasing tension and lasting longer than a normal massage), rolfing (deep massage focused on release of connective tissue), acupuncture, acupressure, craniosacral massage (designed to bring balance to the central nervous system), chiropractic care, and homeopathy (treatment of a disease through minute doses of natural substances).

Chapter 8: The Physical Gut: The Body-Gut Connection

In this chapter, you learn how movement and meditation benefit long-term gut healing and health. Dr. Pedre shares seven daily yoga poses for gut health from yoga teachers and gurus in addition to positive affirmations and breath work. The body-gut connection is about rediscovering the important relationship to our physical bodies, helping create total wellness throughout our body. We need movement to stay healthy and it is also an important part of gut health. Any way you get your body moving is a solid exercise.

Exercise is not only good for your heart and prolonging your life, it is also essential to benefitting your gut's ecosystem living inside of you, promoting a healthy digestive system. Yoga can help you get in touch with your body and improve your gut's functioning. It calms the nervous system promoting healthy digestion. Having a regular meditation and yoga practice deepens your connection to yourself in numerous ways.

Remember to do only what you can physically do and don't push it too far. Be flexible and patient as you will improve over time and with more practice. Dr. Pedre outlines seven yoga poses to help your body and gut that you can incorporate into your daily schedule. Breathing exercises like listening to your breath and reflecting on it and breathing where there is tension in your body can help alleviate the stress present.

Conclusion

After listing a slew of recipes, Dr. Pedre concludes the fifth and final part of Happy Gut with helpful tools and resources. The Appendices include tools to assist you in getting through the program, including food and symptom journals, a health timeline, a post-program questionnaire, recommended supplements, and a list of important resources.

Discussion Questions about Happy Gut

- What is the Happy Gut Diet and what foods can you eat or not eat?

- Why is a happy gut essential to overall health and happiness?

- Why is sugar so bad for you?

- Why does gluten need to be cut out of your diet?

- What does a typical day in the Gut C.A.R.E. Program look like?

- How do you reintroduce foods back into your diet after the 28-day Gut C.A.R.E. Program?

- How do yoga and meditation help alleviate stress and promote a happy and healthy gut?

- How do the mind and gut communicate with each other and why is a healthy gut essential to maintaining a better mood?

- Why is the body-gut connection so crucial to attaining overall wellness?

Author Information about Vincent Pedre, MD

Dr. Vincent Pedre is the medical director of Pedre Integrative Health, a board-certified internist, and a certified Functional Medicine practitioner in private practice in New York City. His integrative medical approach combines both Western and Eastern traditions. He is a clinical instructor at the Mount Sinai School of Medicine and is also certified in yoga and medical acupuncture. Dr. Pedre based his Gut C.A.R.E. Program on his own recovery from irritable bowl syndrome, becoming an expert on healing the body from the inside out. He is also the founder of Dr. Pedre Wellness, which offers health-enhancing programs, content and lifestyle products, dietary supplements, and weight loss programs. He is a sought after speaker at medical conferences around the world.

Made in the USA
Middletown, DE
22 January 2020

83562745R00027